- Begin each day by telling yourself: Today I shall be meeting with interference, ingratitude, insolence, disloyalty, ill-will, and selfishness – all of them due to the offenders' ignorance of what is good or evil. But for my part I have long perceived the nature of good and its nobility, the nature of evil and its meanness, and also the nature of the culprit himself, who is my brother (not in the physical sense, but as a fellow-creature similarly endowed with reason and a share of the divine); therefore none of those things can injure me, for nobody can implicate me in what is degrading. Neither can I be angry with my brother or fall foul of him; for he and I were born to work together, like a man's two hands, feet, or eyelids, or like the upper and lower rows of his teeth. To obstruct each other is against Nature's law – and what is irritation or aversion but a form of obstruction?

- A little flesh, a little breath, and a Reason to rule all – that is myself. As one already on the threshold of death, think nothing of the first – of its viscid blood, its bones, its web of nerves and veins and arteries. The breath, too; what is that? A whiff of wind; and not even the same wind, but every moment puffed out and drawn in anew. But the third, the Reason, the master – on this you must concentrate. Now that your hairs are grey, let it play the part of a slave no more, twitching puppetwise at every pull of self-interest; and cease to fume at destiny by ever grumbling at today or lamenting over tomorrow.

- The whole divine economy is pervaded by Providence. Even the vagaries of chance have their place in Nature's scheme; that is, in the intricate tapestry of the ordinances of Providence. Providence is the source from which all things flow; and allied with it is Necessity, and the welfare of the universe. You yourself are a part of that universe; and for any one of nature's parts, that which is assigned to it by the World-Nature or helps to keep it in being is good. Moreover, what keeps the whole world in being is Change: not merely change of the basic elements, but also change of the larger formations they compose. On these thoughts rest content, and ever hold them as principles. Forget your thirst for books; so that when your end comes you may not murmur, but meet it with a good grace and with unfeigned gratitude in your heart to the gods.

MARCUS
AURELIUS

MEDITATIONS

PENGUIN BOOKS

PENGUIN BOOKS

Published by the Penguin Group. Penguin Books Ltd, 27 Wrights Lane, London w8 5TZ, England. Penguin Books USA Inc, 375 Hudson Street, New York, New York 10014, USA. Penguin Books Australia Ltd, Ringwood, Victoria, Australia. Penguin Books Canada Ltd, 10 Alcorn Avenue, Toronto, Ontario, Canada M4V 3B2. Penguin Books (NZ) Ltd, 182–190 Wairau Road, Auckland 10, New Zealand · Penguin Books Ltd, Registered Offices: Harmondsworth, Middlesex, England · **The complete text of Marcus Aurelius'** *Meditations*, **translated by Maxwell Staniforth, was published by Penguin Books in 1964.** This edition, abridged by Robin Waterfield, published 1995 · Translation copyright © Maxwell Staniforth, 1964. All rights reserved · Typeset by Datix International Limited, Bungay, Suffolk. Printed in England by Clays Ltd, St Ives plc · Except in the United States of America, this book is sold subject to the condition that it shall not, by way of trade or otherwise, be lent, re-sold, hired out, or otherwise circulated without the publisher's prior consent in any form of binding or cover other than that in which it is published and without a similar condition including this condition being imposed on the subsequent purchaser · 10 9 8 7 6 5 4 3 2 1

- Think of your many years of procrastination; how the gods have repeatedly granted you further periods of grace, of which you have taken no advantage. It is time now to realize the nature of the universe to which you belong, and of that controlling Power whose offspring you are; and to understand that your time has a limit set to it. Use it, then, to advance your enlightenment; or it will be gone, and never in your power again.

- Hour by hour resolve firmly to do what comes to hand with correct and natural dignity, and with humanity, independence, and justice. Allow your mind freedom from all other considerations. This you can do, if you will approach each action as though it were your last, dismissing the wayward thought, the emotional recoil from the commands of reason, the desire to create an impression, the admiration of self, the discontent with your lot. See how little a man needs to master, for his days to flow on in quietness and piety: he has but to observe these few counsels, and the gods will ask nothing more.

- Are you distracted by outward cares? Then allow yourself a space of quiet, wherein you can add to your knowledge of the Good and learn to curb your restlessness. Guard also against another kind of error: the folly 3 of those who weary their days in much business, but lack any aim on which their whole effort, nay, their whole thought, is focused.

- In all you do or say or think, recollect that at any time the power of withdrawal from life is in your own hands. If gods exist, you have nothing to fear in taking leave of mankind, for they will not let you come to harm. But if there are no gods, or if they have no concern with mortal affairs, what is life to me, in a world devoid of gods or devoid of Providence? Gods, however, do exist, and do concern themselves with the world of men. They have given us full power not to fall into any of the absolute evils; and if there were real evil in life's other experiences, they would have provided for that too, so that avoidance of it could lie within every man's ability. But when a thing does not worsen the man himself, how can it worsen the life he lives? The World-Nature cannot have been so ignorant as to overlook a hazard of this kind, nor, if aware of it, have been unable to devise a safeguard or a remedy. Neither want of power nor want of skill could have led Nature into the error of allowing good and evil to be visited indiscriminately on the virtuous and the sinful alike. Yet living and dying, honour and dishonour, pain and pleasure, riches and poverty, and so forth are equally the lot of good men and bad. Things like these neither elevate nor degrade; and therefore they are no more good than they are evil.

- Our mental powers should enable us to perceive the swiftness with which all things vanish away: their bodies in the world of space, and their remembrance in the world of time. We should also observe the nature of all objects of sense – particularly such as allure us with pleasure, or affright us with pain, or are clamorously urged upon us by the voice of self-conceit – the cheapness and contemptibility of them, how sordid they are, and how quickly fading and dead. We should discern the true worth of those whose word and opinion confer reputations. We should apprehend, too, the nature of death; and that if only it be steadily contemplated, and the fancies we associate with it be mentally dissected, it will soon come to be thought of as no more than a process of nature – or rather, something more than a mere process, a positive contribution to nature's well-being. Also we can learn how man has contact with God, and with which part of himself this is maintained, and how that part fares after its removal hence.

- Nothing is more melancholy than to compass the whole creation, 'probing into the deeps of earth', as the poet 5 says, and peering curiously into the secrets of others' souls, without once understanding that to hold fast to the divine spirit within, and serve it loyally, is all that is needful. Such service involves keeping it pure from passion, and from aimlessness, and from discontent with the works of gods or men . . .

- Were you to live three thousand years, or even thirty thousand, remember that the sole life which a man can lose is that which he is living at the moment; and furthermore, that he can have no other life except the one he loses. This means that the longest life and the shortest amount to the same thing. For the passing minute is every man's equal possession, but what has once gone by is not ours. Our loss, therefore, is limited to that one fleeting instant, since no one can lose what is already past, nor yet what is still to come – for how can he be deprived of what he does not possess? So two things should be borne in mind. First, that all the cycles of creation since the beginning of time exhibit the same recurring pattern, so that it can make no difference whether you watch the identical spectacle for a hundred years, or for two hundred, or for ever. Secondly, that when the longest- and the shortest-lived of us come to die, their loss is precisely equal. For the sole thing of which any man can be deprived is the present; since this is all he owns, and nobody can lose what is not his.

- For a human soul, the greatest of self-inflicted wrongs is to make itself (so far as it is able to do so) a kind of tumour or abscess on the universe; for to quarrel with circumstances is always a rebellion against Nature – and Nature includes the nature of each individual part. Another wrong, again, is to reject a fellow-creature or oppose him with malicious intent, as men do when they are angry. A third, to surrender to pleasure or pain. A fourth, to dissemble and show insincerity or falsity in word or deed. A fifth, for the soul to direct its acts and endeavours to no particular object, and waste its energies purposelessly and without due thought; for even the least of our activities ought to have some end in view – and for creatures with reason, that end is conformity with the reason and law of the primordial City and Commonwealth.

- In the life of a man, his time is but a moment, his being an incessant flux, his senses a dim rushlight, his body a prey of worms, his soul an unquiet eddy, his fortune dark, and his fame doubtful. In short, all that is of the body is as coursing waters, all that is of the soul as dreams and vapours; life a warfare, a brief sojourning in an alien land; and after repute, oblivion. Where, then, can man find the power to guide and guard his steps? In one thing and one alone: Philosophy. To be a philosopher is to keep unsullied and unscathed the divine spirit within him, so that it may transcend all pleasure and all pain, take nothing in hand without purpose and nothing falsely or with dissimulation, depend not on another's actions or inactions, accept each and every dispensation as coming from the same Source as itself – and last and chief, wait with a good grace for death, as no more than a simple dissolving of the elements whereof each living thing is composed. If those elements themselves take no harm from their ceaseless forming and reforming, why look with mistrust upon the change and dissolution of the whole? It is but Nature's way; and in the ways of Nature there is no evil to be found.

· The daily wearing away of life, with its ever-shrinking remainder, is not the only thing we have to consider. For even if a man's years be prolonged, we must still take into account that it is doubtful whether his mind will continue to retain its capacity for the understanding of business, or for the contemplative effort needed to apprehend things divine and human. The onset of senility may involve no loss of respiratory or alimentary powers, or of sensations, impulses and so forth; nevertheless, the ability to make full use of his faculties, to assess correctly the demands of duty, to coordinate all the diverse problems that arise, to judge if the time has come to end his days on earth, or to make any other of the decisions that require the exercise of a practised intellect, is already on the wane. We must press on, then, in haste; not simply because every hour brings us nearer to death, but because even before then our powers of perception and comprehension begin to deteriorate.

· Thus to a man of sensitiveness and sufficiently deep insight into the workings of the universe, almost everything, even if it be no more than a by-product of something else, seems to add its meed of extra pleasure. Such a man will view the grinning jaws of real lions and tigers as admiringly as he would an artist's or sculptor's imitation of them; and the eye of discretion will enable him to see the mature charm that belongs to men and women in old age, as well as the seductive bloom that is youth's. Things of this sort will not appeal to everyone; he alone who has cultivated a real intimacy with Nature and her works will be struck by them.

· Hippocrates cured the ills of many, but himself took ill and died. The Chaldeans foretold the deaths of many, but fate caught up with them also. Alexander, Pompey, and Julius Caesar laid waste whole cities time and again, and cut down many thousands of horse and foot in battle, but the hour came when they too passed away. And the moral of it all? This. You embark; you make the voyage; you reach port: step ashore, then. Into another life? There are gods everywhere, even yonder. Into final insensibility? Then you will be out of the grip of pains and pleasures, and thrall no longer to this earthen vessel, so immeasurably meaner than its attendant minister. For the one is a mind and a divinity; the other but clay and corruption.

- Do not waste what remains of your life in speculating about your neighbours, unless with a view to some mutual benefit. To wonder what so-and-so is doing and why, or what he is saying, or thinking, or scheming – in a word, anything that distracts you from fidelity to the Ruler within you – means a loss of opportunity for some other task. See then that the flow of your thoughts is kept free from idle or random fancies, particularly those of an inquisitive or uncharitable nature. A man should habituate himself to such a way of thinking that if suddenly asked, 'What is in your mind at this minute?' he could respond frankly and without hesitation; thus proving that all his thoughts were simple and kindly, as becomes a social being with no taste for the pleasures of sensual imaginings, jealousies, envies, suspicions, or any other sentiments that he would blush to acknowledge in himself. Such a man, determined here and now to aspire to the heights, is indeed a priest and minister of the gods; for he is making full use of that indwelling power which can keep a man unsullied by pleasures, proof against pain, untouched by insult, and impervious to evil. He is a competitor in the greatest of all contests, the struggle against passion's mastery; he is imbued through and through with uprightness, welcoming whole-heartedly whatever falls to his lot and rarely asking himself what others may be saying or doing or thinking except when the public interest requires it. He confines his operations to his own concerns, having his attentions fixed on his own particular thread of the universal web; seeing to it that his actions are honour-able, and convinced that what befalls him must be for the best – for his own directing fate is itself under a higher direction. He does not forget the brotherhood of all rational beings, nor that a concern for every man is proper to humanity; and he knows that it is not the world's opinions he should follow, but only those of men whose lives confessedly accord with Nature. As for others whose lives are not so ordered, he reminds himself constantly of the characters they exhibit daily and nightly at home and abroad, and of the sort of society they frequent; and the approval of such men, who do not even stand well in their own eyes, has no value for him.

- In your actions let there be a willing promptitude, yet a regard for the common interest; due deliberation, yet no irresolution; and in your sentiments no pretentious over-refinement. Avoid talkativeness, avoid officiousness. The god within you should preside over a being who is virile and mature, a statesman, a Roman, and a ruler; one who has held his ground, like a soldier waiting for the signal to retire from life's battlefield and ready to welcome his relief; a man whose credit need neither be sworn to by himself nor avouched by others. Therein is the secret of cheerfulness, of depending on no help from without and needing to crave from no man the boon of tranquillity. We have to stand upright ourselves, not be set up.

- If mortal life can offer you anything better than justice and truth, self-control and courage – that is, peace of mind in the evident conformity of your actions to the laws of reason, and peace of mind under the visitations of a destiny you cannot control – if, I say, you can discern any higher ideal, why, turn to it with your whole soul, and rejoice in the prize you have found. But if nothing seems to you better than the deity which dwells within you, directing each impulse, weighing each impression, abjuring (in the Socratic phrase) the temptations of the flesh, and avowing allegiance to the gods and compassion for mankind; if you find all else to be mean and worthless in comparison, then leave yourself no room for any rival pursuits. For if you once falter and turn aside, you will no longer be able to give unswerving loyalty to this ideal you have chosen for your own. No ambitions of a different nature can contest the title to goodness which belongs to reason and civic duty; not the world's applause, nor power, nor wealth, nor the enjoyment of pleasure. For a while there may seem to be no incongruity in these things, but very quickly they get the upper hand and sweep a man off his balance.

· Never value the advantages derived from anything involving breach of faith, loss of self-respect, hatred, suspicion, or execration of others, insincerity, or the desire for something which has to be veiled and curtained. One whose chief regard is for his own mind, and for the divinity within him and the service of its goodness, will strike no poses, utter no complaints, and crave neither for solitude nor yet for a crowd. Best of 13 all, his life will be free from continual pursuings and avoidings. He does not care whether his soul in its mortal frame shall be his to possess for a longer or a shorter term of years; this very moment, if it be the hour for his departure, he will step forth as readily as he performs another act that can be done in self-respecting and orderly fashion. No other care has he in life but to keep his mind from straying into paths incompatible with those of an intelligent and social being.

- Treat with respect the power you have to form an opinion. By it alone can the helmsman within you avoid forming opinions that are at variance with nature and with the constitution of a reasonable being. From it you may look to attain circumspection, good relations with your fellow-men, and conformity with the will of heaven.

- Letting go all else, cling to the following few truths. Remember that man lives only in the present, in this fleeting instant: all the rest of his life is either past and gone, or not yet revealed. This mortal life is a little thing, lived in a little corner of the earth; and little, too, is the longest fame to come – dependent as it is on a succession of fast-perishing little men who have no knowledge even of their own selves, much less of one long dead and gone.

- If you do the task before you always adhering to strict reason with zeal and energy and yet with humanity, disregarding all lesser ends and keeping the divinity within you pure and upright, as though you were even now faced with its recall – if you hold steadily to this, staying for nothing and shrinking from nothing, only seeking in each passing action a conformity with nature and in each word and utterance a fearless truthfulness, then shall the good life be yours. And from this course no man has the power to hold you back.

- Body, soul, and mind: the body for sensation, the soul for the springs of action, the mind for principles. Yet the capacity for sensation belongs also to the stalled ox; there is no wild beast or degenerate but obeys the twitchings of impulse; and even men who deny the gods, or betray their country, or perpetrate all manner of villainy behind locked doors, have minds to guide them to the clear path of duty. Seeing, then, that all else is in common heritage of such types, the good man's only singularity lies in his approving welcome to every experience the looms of fate may weave for him, his refusal to soil the divinity seated in his breast or perturb it with disorderly impressions, and his resolve to keep it in serenity and decorous obedience to God, admitting no disloyalty to truth in his speech or to justice in his actions. Though all the world mistrust him because he lives in simple, self-respecting happiness, he takes offence at none, but unswervingly treads the road onward to life's close, where duty bids him arrive in purity and peace, unreluctant to depart, in perfect and unforced unison with fate's apportionment.

• If the inward power that rules us be true to Nature, it will always adjust itself readily to the possibilities and opportunities offered by circumstance. It asks for no predeterminate material; in the pursuance of its aims it is willing to compromise; hindrances to its progress are merely converted into matter for its own use. It is like a bonfire mastering a heap of rubbish, which would have quenched a feeble glow; but its fiery blaze quickly assimilates the load, consumes it, and flames the higher for it.

• Men seek for seclusion in the wilderness, by the seashore, or in the mountains – a dream you have cherished only too fondly yourself. But such fancies are wholly unworthy of a philosopher, since at any moment you choose you can retire within yourself. Nowhere can man find a quieter or more untroubled retreat than in his own soul; above all, he who possesses resources in himself, which he need only contemplate to secure immediate ease of mind – the ease that is but another word for a well-ordered spirit. Avail yourself often, then, of this retirement, and so continually renew yourself. Make your rules of life brief, yet so as to embrace the fundamentals; recurrence to them will suffice to remove all vexation, and send you back without fretting to the duties to which you must return.

After all, what is it that frets you? The vices of humanity? Remember the doctrine that all rational beings are created for one another; that toleration is a part of justice; and that men are not intentional evildoers. Think of the myriad enmities, suspicions, animosities, and conflicts that are now vanished with the dust and ashes of the men who knew them; and fret no more.

Or is it your allotted portion in the universe that chafes you? Recall once again the dilemma, 'if not a wise Providence, then a mere jumble of atoms', and consider the profusion of evidence that this world is as it were a city. Do the ills of the body afflict you? Reflect that the mind has but to detach itself and apprehend its own powers, to be no longer involved with the movements of the breath, whether they be smooth or rough. In short, recollect all you have learnt and accepted regarding pain and pleasure.

Or does the bubble reputation distract you? Keep before your eyes the swift onset of oblivion, and the abysses of eternity before us and behind; mark how hollow are the echoes of applause, how fickle and undiscerning the judgements of professed admirers, and how puny the arena of human fame. For the entire earth is but a point, and the place of our own habitation but a minute corner in it; and how many are therein who will praise you, and what sort of men are they?

Remember then to withdraw into the little field of self. Above all, never struggle or strain; but be master of yourself, and view life as a man, as a human being, as a citizen, and as a mortal. Among the truths you will do well to contemplate most frequently are these two: first, that things can never touch the soul, but stand inert outside it, so that disquiet can arise only from fancies within; and secondly, that all visible objects change in a moment, and will be no more. Think of the countless changes in which you yourself have had a part. The whole universe is change, and life itself is but what you deem it.

· If the power of thought is universal among mankind, so

likewise is the possession of reason, making us rational

creatures. It follows, therefore, that this reason speaks no less universally to us all with its 'thou shalt' or 'thou shalt not'. So then there is a world-law; which in turn means that we are all fellow-citizens and share a common citizenship, and that the world is a single city. Is there any other common citizenship that can be claimed by all humanity? And it is from this world-polity that mind, reason, and law themselves derive. If not, whence else? As the earthy portion of me has its origin from earth, the watery from a different element, my breath from one source and my hot and fiery parts from another of their own elsewhere (for nothing comes from nothing, or can return to nothing), so too there must be an origin for the mind.

· That men of a certain type should behave as they do is inevitable. To wish it otherwise were to wish the fig-tree would not yield its juice. In any case, remember that in a very little while both you and he will be dead, and your very names will quickly be forgotten.

· Put from you the belief that 'I have been wronged', and with it will go the feeling. Reject your sense of injury, and the injury itself disappears.

· Whatever happens, happens rightly. Watch closely, and

you will find this true. In the succession of events there is not mere sequence alone, but an order that is just and right, as from the hand of one who dispenses to all their due. Keep up your watch, then, as you have begun, and let goodness accompany your every action – goodness, that is, in the proper sense of the word. In all your operations pay heed to this.

- At two points hold yourself always in readiness: first, to do exclusively what reason, our king and lawgiver, shall suggest for the common weal; and secondly, to reconsider a decision if anyone present should correct you and convince you of an error of judgement. But such conviction must proceed from the assurance that justice, or the common good, or some other such interest will be served. This must be the sole consideration; not the likelihood of pleasure or popularity.

- The man whose heart is palpitating for fame after death does not reflect that out of all those who remember him every one will himself soon be dead also, and in course of time the next generation after that, until in the end, after flaring and sinking by turns, the final spark of memory is quenched. Furthermore, even supposing that those who remember you were never to die at all, nor their memories to die either, yet what is that to you?

Clearly, in your grave, nothing; and even in your life-time, what is the good of praise – unless maybe to sub-serve some lesser design? Surely, then, you are making an inopportune rejection of what Nature has given you today, if all your mind is set on what men will say of you tomorrow.

- Anything in any way beautiful derives its beauty from itself, and asks nothing beyond itself. Praise is no part of it, for nothing is made worse or better by praise. This applies even to the more mundane forms of beauty: natural objects, for example, or works of art. What need has true beauty of anything further? Surely none; any more than law, or truth, or kindness, or modesty. Is any of these embellished by praise, or spoiled by censure? Does the emerald lose its beauty for lack of admiration? Does gold, or ivory, or purple? A lyre or a dagger, a rosebud or a sapling?

- Never allow yourself to be swept off your feet: when an impulse stirs, see first that it will meet the claims of justice; when an impression forms, assure yourself first of its certainty.

- 'If thou wouldst know contentment, let thy deeds be few,' said the sage. Better still, limit them strictly to such as are essential, and to such as in a social being reason demands, and as it demands. This brings the contentment that comes of doing a few things and doing them well. Most of what we say and do is not necessary, and its omission would save both time and trouble. At every step, therefore, a man should ask himself, 'Is this one of the things that are superfluous?' Moreover, not idle actions only but even idle impressions ought to be suppressed; for then unnecessary action will not ensue.

· If he who knows not what is in the universe is a stranger to the universe, he is no less so who knows not what takes place in it. Such a man is an exile, self-banished from the polity of reason; a sightless man, having the eyes of his understanding darkened; a pauper dependent on others, without resources of his own for his livelihood. He is an excrescence on the world, when he dissociates and dissevers himself from the laws of our common nature by refusing to accept his lot (which after all is a product of the self-same Nature which produced yourself); he is a limb lopped from the community, when he cuts his own soul adrift from the single soul of all rational things.

22 · Give your heart to the trade you have learnt, and draw

refreshment from it. Let the rest of your days be spent as one who has whole-heartedly committed his all to the gods, and is thenceforth no man's master or slave.

- Expressions that were once current have gone out of use nowadays. Names, too, that were formerly household worlds are virtually archaisms today. All things fade into the storied past, and in a little while are shrouded in oblivion. Even to men whose lives were a blaze of glory this comes to pass; as for the rest, the breath is hardly out of them before, in Homer's words, they are 'lost to sight alike and hearsay'. What, after all, is immortal fame? An empty, hollow thing. To what, then, must we aspire? This, and this alone: the just thought, the unselfish act, the tongue that utters no falsehood, the temper that greets each passing event as something predestined, expected, and emanating from the One source and origin.

- Observe how all things are continually being born of change; teach yourself to see that Nature's highest happiness lies in changing the things that are, and forming new things after their kind. Whatever is, is in some sense the seed of what is to emerge from it. Nothing can become a philosopher less than to imagine that seed can only be something that is planted in the earth or the womb.

• For you, evil comes not from the mind of another; nor yet from any of the phases and changes of your own bodily frame. Then whence? From that part of yourself which acts as your assessor of what is evil. Refuse its assessment, and all is well. Though the poor body, so closely neighbouring it, be gashed or burned, fester or mortify, let the voice of this assessor remain silent; let it pronounce nothing to be bad or good if it can happen to evil men and good men alike – for anything that comes impartially upon men, whether they observe the rules of Nature or not, can neither be hindering her purposes nor advancing them.

• Always think of the universe as one living organism, with a single substance and a single soul; and observe how all things are submitted to the single perceptivity of this one whole, all are moved by its single impulse, and all play their part in the causation of every event that happens. Remark the intricacy of the skein, the complexity of the web.

• To be in process of change is not an evil, any more than to be the product of change is a good.

- Time is a river, the resistless flow of all created things. One thing no sooner comes in sight than it is hurried past and another is borne along, only to be swept away in its turn.

- Everything that happens is as normal and expected as the spring rose or the summer fruit; this is true of sickness, death, slander, intrigue, and all the other things that delight or trouble foolish men.

- What follows is ever closely linked to what precedes; it is not a procession of isolated events, merely obeying the laws of sequence, but a rational continuity. Moreover, just as the things already in existence are all harmoniously coordinated, things in the act of coming into existence exhibit the same marvel of concatenation, rather than simply the bare fact of succession.

- Remind yourself constantly of all the physicians, now dead, who used to knit their brows over their ailing patients; of all the astrologers who so solemnly predicted their clients' doom; the philosophers who expatiated so endlessly on death or immortality; the great commanders who slew their thousands; the despots who wielded powers of life and death with such terrible arrogance, as if themselves were gods who could never die; the whole

25

cities which have perished completely, Helice, Pompeii, Herculaneum, and others without number. After that, recall one by one each of your own acquaintances; how one buried another, only to be laid low himself and buried in turn by a third, and all in so brief a space of time. Observe, in short, how transient and trivial is all mortal life; yesterday a drop of semen, tomorrow a handful of spice or ashes. Spend, therefore, these fleeting moments on earth as Nature would have you spend them, and then go to your rest with a good grace, as an olive falls in its season, with a blessing for the earth that bore it and a thanksgiving to the tree that gave it life.

- Be like the headland against which the waves break and break: it stands firm, until presently the watery tumult around it subsides once more to rest. 'How unlucky I am, that this should have happened to me!' By no means; say rather, 'How lucky I am that it has left me with no bitterness; unshaken by the present, and undismayed by the future.' The thing could have happened to anyone, but not everyone would have emerged unembittered. So why put the one down to misfortune, rather than the other to good fortune? Can a man call anything at all a misfortune, if it is not a contravention of his nature; and can it be a contravention of his nature if it is not against that nature's will? Well, then:

you have learnt to know that will. Does this thing which has happened hinder you from being just, magnanimous, temperate, judicious, discreet, truthful, self-respecting, independent, and all else by which a man's nature comes to its fulfilment? So here is a rule to remember in future, when anything tempts you to feel bitter: not, 'This is a misfortune,' but 'To bear this worthily is good fortune.'

- Ever run the short way; and the short way is the way of nature, with perfect soundness in each word and deed as the goal. Such an aim will give you freedom from anxiety and strife, and from all compromise and artifice.

- At day's first light have in readiness, against disinclination to leave your bed, the thought that 'I am rising for the work of man'. Must I grumble at setting out to do what I was born for, and for the sake of which I have been brought into the world? Is this the purpose of my creation, to lie here under the blankets and keep myself warm? 'Ah, but it is a great deal more pleasant!' Was it for pleasure, then, that you were born, and not for work, not for effort? Look at the plants, the sparrows, ants, spiders, bees, all busy at their own tasks, each doing his part towards a coherent world-order; and will you refuse man's share of the work, instead of being prompt to carry out Nature's bidding? 'Yes, but one must have some repose as well.' Granted; but repose has its limits set by nature, in the same way as food and drink have; and you overstep these limits, you go beyond the point of sufficiency; while on the other hand, when action is in question, you stop short of what you could well achieve.

You have no real love for yourself; if you had, you would love your nature, and your nature's will. Craftsmen who love their trade will spend themselves to the utmost in labouring at it, even going unwashed and unfed; but you hold your nature in less regard than the engraver does his engraving, the dancer his dancing, the miser his heap of silver, or the vainglorious man his moment of glory. These men, when their heart is in it, are ready to sacrifice food and sleep to the advancement of their chosen pursuit. Is the service of the community of less worth in your eyes, and does it merit less devotion?

• There is a type of person who, if he renders you a service, has no hesitation in claiming the credit for it. Another, though not prepared to go so far as that, will nevertheless secretly regard you as in his debt and be fully conscious of what he has done. But there is also the man who, one might almost say, has no conscious-ness at all of what he has done, like the vine which produces a cluster of grapes and then, having yielded its rightful fruit, looks for no more thanks than a horse that has run his race, a hound that has traced his quarry, or a bee that has hived her honey. Like them, the man who has done one good action does not cry it aloud, but passes straight on to a second, as the vine passes on to the bearing of another summer's grapes.

- Just as we say 'A doctor has prescribed horseback exercise, or cold baths, or going barefoot,' so in the same way does the World-Nature prescribe disease, mutilation, loss, or some other disability. In the former case, prescribing meant ordering a specific treatment, in the interests of the patient's health; similarly in the latter, certain specific occurrences are ordered, in the interests of our destiny. We may, in fact, be said to 'meet with' these misfortunes in the same sense as masons say that the squared stones in walls or pyramids 'meet with' each other when they are being fitted closely together to make the unified whole. This mutual integration is a universal principle. As a myriad bodies combine into the single Body which is the world, so a myriad causes combine into the single Cause which is destiny. Even the common people realize this when they say, 'It was brought upon him.' It was indeed brought upon him; that is, it was prescribed for him. Let us accept such things, then, as we accept the prescriptions of a doctor; for they, too, have often a harsh flavour, yet we swallow them gladly in hope of health. The execution and fulfilment of Nature's decrees should be viewed in the same way as we view our bodily health: even if what befalls is unpalatable, nevertheless always receive it gladly, for it makes for the health of the universe, and even for the well-being and well-doing of Zeus himself. Had it not been for the benefit of the whole, he would never have brought it upon the individual. It is not Nature's way to bring anything upon that which is under her government, except what is specifically designed for its good. There are two reasons, then, why you should willingly accept what happens to you: first, because it happens to yourself, has been prescribed for yourself, and concerns yourself, being a strand in the tapestry of primordial causation; and secondly, because every individual dispensation is one of the causes of the prosperity, success, and even survival of That which administers the universe. To break off any particle, no matter how small, from the continuous concatenation – whether of causes or of any other elements – is to injure the whole. And each time you give way to discontent, you are causing, within your own limited ability, just such a breakage and disruption.

* Do not be distressed, do not despond or give up in despair, if now and again practice falls short of precept. Return to the attack after each failure, and be thankful if on the whole you can acquit yourself in the majority of cases as a man should. But have a genuine liking for the discipline you return to: do not recur to your philosophy in the spirit of a schoolboy to his master, but as the sore-eyed recur to their egg-and-sponge lotion, or as others to their poultice or their douche. In this way your submission to reason will not become a matter for public display, but for private consolation.

* Unless things pertain to a man, as man, they cannot properly be said to belong to him. They cannot be required of him; for his nature neither promises them, nor is perfected by them. Therefore they cannot represent his chief end in life, not even the 'good' which is the means to that end. Moreover, had man's natural heritage included such things, it could not at the same time have included contempt and renunciation of them; nor would the ability to do without them have been any cause for commendation; nor, supposing them to be really good, would failure to claim a full share of them

be compatible with goodness. As it is, however, the more a man deprives himself, or submits to be deprived, of such things and their like, the more he grows in goodness.

- To pursue the unattainable is insanity, yet the thoughtless can never refrain from doing so.

- Nothing can happen to any man that nature has not fitted him to endure. Your neighbour's experiences are no different from your own; yet he, being either less aware of what has happened or more eager to show his mettle, stands steady and undaunted. For shame, that ignorance and vanity should prove stronger than wisdom!

- Outward things can touch the soul not a whit; they know no way into it, they have no power to sway or move it. By itself it sways and moves itself; it has its own self-approved standards of judgement, and to them it refers every experience.

- In one way humanity touches me very nearly, inasmuch as I am bound to do good to my fellow-creatures and bear with them. On the other hand, to the extent that individual men hamper my proper activities, humanity becomes a thing as indifferent to me as the sun, the wind, or the creatures of the wild. True, others may hinder the carrying out of certain actions; but they cannot obstruct my will, nor the disposition of my mind, since these will always safeguard themselves under reservations and adapt themselves to circumstances. The mind can circumvent all obstacles to action, and turn them to the furtherance of its main purpose, so that any impediment to its work becomes instead an auxiliary, and the barriers in its path become aids to progress.

· In the universe, reverence that which is highest: namely, That to which all else ministers, and which gives the law to all. In like manner, too, reverence the highest in yourself: it is of one piece with the Other, since in yourself also it is that to which all the rest minister, and by which your life is directed.

· Reflect often upon the rapidity with which all existing things, or things coming into existence, sweep past us and are carried away. The great river of Being flows on without a pause; its actions for ever changing, its causes shifting endlessly, hardly a single thing standing still; while ever at hand looms infinity stretching behind and before – the abyss in which all things are lost to sight. 33

In such conditions, surely a man were foolish to gasp and fume and fret, as though the time of his troubling could ever be of long continuance.

- Think of the totality of all Being, and what a mite of it is yours; think of all Time, and the brief fleeting instant of it that is allotted to yourself; think of Destiny, and how puny a part of it you are.

- Is one doing me wrong? Let himself look to that; his humours and his actions are his own. As for me, I am only receiving what the World-Nature wills me to receive, and acting as my own nature wills me to act.

- Let no emotions of the flesh, be they of pain or pleasure, affect the supreme and sovereign portion of the soul. See that it never becomes involved with them: it must limit itself to its own domain, and keep the feelings confined to their proper sphere. If (through the sympathy which permeates any unified organism) they do spread to the mind, there need be no attempt to resist the physical sensation; only, the master-reason must refrain from adding its own assumptions of their goodness or badness.

34 • Live with the gods. To live with the gods is to show

them at all times a soul contented with their awards, and wholly fulfilling the will of that inward divinity, that particle of himself, which Zeus has given to every man for ruler and guide – the mind and the reason.

- It is possible to live on earth as you mean to live hereafter. But if men will not let you, then quit the house of life; though not with any feeling of ill-usage. 'The hut smokes; I move out.' No need to make a great business of it. Nevertheless, so long as nothing of the kind obliges me to depart, here I remain, my own master, and none shall hinder me from doing what I choose – and what I choose is to live the life that nature enjoins for a reasonable member of a social community.

- The Mind of the universe is social. At all events, it has created the lower forms to serve the higher, and then linked together the higher in a mutual dependence on each other. Observe how some are subjected, others are connected, each and all are given their just due, and the more eminent among them are combined in mutual accord.

- In a brief while now you will be ashes or bare bones; a name, or perhaps not even a name – though even a name is no more than empty sound and reiteration. All that men set their hearts on in this life is vanity, corruption, and trash; men are like scuffling puppies, or quarrelsome children who are all smiles one moment and in tears the next.

- Press on steadily, keep to the straight road in your thinking and doing, and your days will ever flow on smoothly. The soul of man, like the souls of all rational creatures, has two things in common with the soul of God: it can never be thwarted from without, and its good consists in righteousness of character and action, and in confining every wish thereto.

- Matter in the universe is supple and compliant, and the Reason which controls it has no motive for ill-doing; for it is without malice, and does nothing with intent to injure, neither is anything harmed by it. By its ordinances all things have their birth and fulfilment.

- If you are doing what is right, never mind whether you are freezing with cold or beside a good fire; heavy-eyed, or fresh from a sound sleep; reviled or applauded; in the act of dying, or about some other piece of business. (For even dying is part of the business of life; and there too no more is required of us than 'to see the moment's work well done'.)

- Look beneath the surface: never let a thing's intrinsic quality or worth escape you.

- All material objects swiftly change: either by sublimation (if the substance of the universe be indeed a unity), or else by dispersion.

- Reason, the controller, has a perfect understanding of the conditions, the purpose, and the materials of its work.

- To refrain from imitation is the best revenge.

- Let your one delight and refreshment be to pass from one service to the community to another, with God ever in mind.

- Our master-reason is something which is both self-awakened and self-directed. It cannot only make itself what it will, but also impose the aspect of its choice on anything which it experiences.

- All things come to their fulfilment as the one universal Nature directs; for there is no rival nature, whether containing her from without, or itself contained within her, or even existing apart and detached from her.

- When force of circumstance upsets your equanimity, lose no time in recovering your self-control, and do not remain out of tune longer than you can help. Habitual recurrence to the harmony will increase your mastery of it.

- One thing hastens into being, another hastens out of it. Even while a thing is in the act of coming into existence, some part of it has already ceased to be. Flux and change are for ever renewing the fabric of the universe, just as the ceaseless sweep of time is for ever renewing the face of eternity. In such a running river, where there is no firm foothold, what is there for a man to value among all the many things that are racing past him? It would be like setting the affections on some sparrow flitting by, which in the selfsame moment is lost to sight.

- Because a thing is difficult for you, do not therefore suppose it to be beyond mortal power. On the contrary, if anything is possible and proper for man to do, assume that it must fall within your own capacity.

- When an opponent in the gymnasium gashes us with his nails or bruises our head in a collision, we do not protest or take offence, and we do not suspect him ever afterwards of malicious intent. However, we do regard him with a wary eye; not in enmity or suspicion, yet good-temperedly keeping our distance,. So let it be, too, at other times in life; let us agree to overlook a great many things in those who are, as it were, our fellow-contestants. A simple avoidance, as I have said, is always open to us, without either suspicion or ill-will.

• If anyone can show me, and prove to me, that I am wrong in thought or deed, I will gladly change. I seek the truth, which never yet hurt anybody. It is only persistence in self-delusion and ignorance which does harm.

• I do that which it is my duty to do. Nothing else distracts me; for it will be either something that is inanimate and irrational, or somebody who is misled and ignorant of the way.

• Be generous and liberal in your attitude to irrational creatures and to the generality of material things, for you have reason and they have none. Human beings, on the other hand, have reason; so treat them in a spirit of fellowship.

• In death, Alexander of Macedon's end differed no whit

from his stable-boy's. Either both were received into the same generative principle of the universe, or both alike were dispersed into atoms.

- Think of the number of things, bodily and mental, that are going on at the same moment within each one of us; and then it will not surprise you that an infinitely greater number of things – everything, in fact, that comes to birth in this vast One-and-All we call the universe – can exist simultaneously therein.

- How barbarous, to deny men the privilege of pursuing what they imagine to be their proper concerns and interests! Yet, in a sense, this is just what you are doing when you allow your indignation to rise at their wrongdoing; for after all, they are only following their own apparent concerns and interests. You say they are mistaken? Why then, tell them so, and explain it to them, instead of being indignant.

- Death: a release from impressions of sense, from twitchings of appetite, from excursions of thought, and from service to the flesh.

- Notice how common artificers will meet the wishes of an unskilled employer up to a certain point, but none the less stand fast by the rules of their trade and refuse to depart from them. Is it not deplorable that a builder or a physician should have more respect for the canons of his craft than man has for his own, which he shares with the gods?

- In the universe Asia and Europe are but two small corners, all ocean's waters a drop, Athos a puny lump of earth, the vastness of time a pin's point in eternity. All is petty, inconstant, and perishable. All proceeds from the one source, springing either directly or derivatively from the universal sovereign Reason. Even the lion's open jaws, the deadly poison, and all other things that do hurt, down to the bramble-bush and the slough, are by-products of something else that is itself noble and beautiful. Do not think of them, then, as alien to That which you reverence, but remember the one origin that is common to them all.

- To see the things of the present moment is to see all that is now, all that has been since time began, and all that shall be unto the world's end; for all things are of one kind and one form.

- Adapt yourself to the environment in which your lot

has been cast, and show true love to the fellow-mortals with whom destiny has surrounded you.

- All is well with a tool, instrument, or utensil when it serves the use for which it was made, though in this case its maker is not present. But with things formed by Nature, the power that fashioned them is still within them, and remains in them. All the more, then, should you have it in reverence, and be assured that if only you live and act according to its will, you have all things to your liking. That is the way in which the universe, too, has all things to its liking.

- If you suppose anything over which you have no control to be either good or bad for you, then the accident of missing the one or encountering the other is certain to make you aggrieved with the gods, and bitter against the men whom you know or suspect to be responsible for your failure or misfortune. We do, in fact, commit many injustices through attaching importance to things of this class. But when we limit our notions of good and evil strictly to what is within our own power, there remains no reason either to bring accusations against God or to set ourselves at variance with men.

• All that befalls the individual is for the good of the

whole. That by itself is warrant enough for us; but if you look closely you will also notice that, as a general rule, what is good for one man is good for his fellowmen as well. ('Good', though, must be taken here in the more popular sense, as inclusive of things that are morally indifferent.)

· When you would have a cordial for your spirits, think of the good qualities of your friends: this one's capability, that one's self-effacement, another's generosity, and so forth. There is no surer remedy for dejection than to see examples of the different virtues displayed in the characters of those around us, exhibiting themselves as plenteously as can be. Wherefore keep them ever before you.

· Try to move men by persuasion; yet act against their will if the principles of justice so direct. But if someone uses force to obstruct you, then take a different line; resign yourself without a pang, and turn the obstacle into an opportunity for the exercise of some other virtue. Your attempt was always subject to reservations, remember; you were not aiming at the impossible. At what, then? Simply at making the attempt itself. In this you succeeded; and with that, the object of your existence is attained.

- The man of ambition thinks to find his good in the operations of others; the man of pleasure in his own sensations; but the man of understanding in his own actions.

- Accustom yourself to give careful attention to what others are saying, and try your best to enter into the mind of the speaker.

- What is evil? A thing you have seen times out of number. Likewise with every other sort of occurrence also, be prompt to remind yourself that this, too, you have witnessed many times before. For everywhere, above and below, you will find nothing but the self-same things; they fill the pages of all history, ancient, modern, and contemporary; and they fill our cities and homes today. There is no such thing as novelty; all is as trite as it is transitory.

- An empty pageant; a stage play; flocks of sheep, herds of cattle; a tussle of spearmen; a bone flung among a pack of curs; a crumb tossed into a pond of fish; ants, loaded and labouring; mice, scared and scampering; puppets, jerking on their strings – that is life. In the midst of it all you must take your stand, good-temperedly and without disdain, yet always aware that a man's worth is no greater than the worth of his ambitions.

- Never let the future disturb you. You will meet it, if you have to, with the same weapons of reason which today arm you against the present.

- All things are interwoven with one another; a sacred bond unites them; there is scarcely one thing that is isolated from another. Everything is coordinated, everything works together in giving form to the one universe. The world-order is a unity made up of multiplicity; God is one, pervading all things; all being is one, all law is one (namely, the common reason which all thinking creatures possess) and all truth is one – if, as we believe, there can be but one path to perfection for beings that are alike in kind and reason.

- Swiftly each particle of matter vanishes into the universal Substance; swiftly each item of causation is reassumed into the Universal Reason; swiftly the remembrance of all things is buried in the gulf of eternity.

- To a reasoning being, an act that accords with nature is an act that accords with reason.

- Whatever the world may say or do, my part is to keep myself good; just as a gold piece, or an emerald, or a 45 purple robe insists perpetually, 'Whatever the world may say or do, my part is to remain an emerald and keep my colour true.'

• We shrink from change; yet is there anything that can come into being without it? What does Nature hold dearer, or more proper to herself? Could you have a hot bath unless the firewood underwent some change? Could you be nourished if the food suffered no change? Is it possible for any useful thing to be achieved without change? Do you not see, then, that change in yourself is of the same order, and no less necessary to Nature?

• It is man's peculiar distinction to love even those who err and go astray. Such a love is born as soon as you realize that they are your brothers; that they are stumbling in ignorance, and not wilfully; that in a short while both of you will be no more; and, above all, that you yourself have taken no hurt, for your master-reason has not been made a jot worse than it was before.

• Out of the universal substance, as out of wax, Nature fashions a colt, then breaks him up and uses the material to form a tree, and after that a man, and next some other thing; and not one of these endures for more than a brief span. As for the vessel itself, it is no greater hardship to be taken to pieces than to be put together.

• An angry look on the face is wholly against nature. If it be assumed frequently, beauty begins to perish, and in the end is quenched beyond rekindling. You must try to realize that this shows the unreasonableness of it; for if we lose the ability to perceive our faults, what is the good of living on?

• When anyone offends against you, let your first thought be, Under what conception of good and ill was this committed? Once you know that, astonishment and anger will give place to pity. For either your own ideas of what is good are no more advanced than his, or at least bear some likeness to them, in which case it is clearly your duty to pardon him; or else, on the other hand, you have grown beyond supposing such actions to be either good or bad, and therefore it will be so much the easier to be tolerant of another's blindness.

• Do not indulge in dreams of having what you have not, but reckon up the chief of the blessings you do possess, and then thankfully remember how you would crave for them if they were not yours. At the same time, however, beware lest delight in them leads you to cherish them so dearly that their loss would destroy your peace of mind.

- Withdraw into yourself. Our master-reason asks no more than to act justly, and thereby to achieve calm.

- Do away with all fancies. Cease to be passion's puppet. Limit time to the present. Learn to recognize every experience for what it is, whether it be your own or another's. Divide and classify the objects of sense into cause and matter. Meditate upon your last hour. Leave your neighbour's wrongdoing to rest with him who initiated it.

- Survey the circling stars, as though yourself were in mid-course with them. Often picture the changing and rechanging dance of the elements. Visions of this kind purge away the dross of our earth-bound life.

- If a deed can be accomplished to accord with that reason which men share with gods, there is nothing to fear. Where a chance of service presents itself, by some action that will go smoothly forward in obedience to the laws of our being, we need look for no harm.

- Cast no side-glance at the instincts governing other men,

but keep your eyes fixed on the goal whereto nature herself guides you – the World-Nature speaking through circumstance, and your own nature speaking through the calls of duty. The acts of man should accord with his natural constitution; and while all other created things are constituted for the service of rational beings (in accordance with the general law by which the lower exists for the good of the higher), these latter are constituted to serve one another. Chief of all features in a man's constitution, therefore, is his duty to his kind. Next after that comes his obligation to resist the murmurs of the flesh; for it is the particular office of his reason and intellect to maintain such a fence around their own workings that they are not overborne by those of the senses or the impulses, both of which are animal in quality. Mind demands the premier place, and will not bow to their yoke; and rightly so, since nature has formed it to make use of all the rest. And thirdly, the constitution of a rational being should make him incapable of indiscretion, and proof against imposture. Let but Reason, the helmsman, steer a straight course, holding fast by these three principles, and be sure it will come by its own.

· Take it that you have died today, and your life's story is ended; and henceforward regard what further time may be given you as an uncovenanted surplus, and live it out in harmony with nature.

- Love nothing but that which comes to you woven in the pattern of your destiny. For what could more aptly fit your needs?

- Dig within. There lies the well-spring of good: ever dig, and it will ever flow.

- Also let your bodily carriage be firm, and without contortions, whether in motion or at rest. As the mind reveals itself in the face, by keeping the features composed and decent, so the same should be required of it in respect of the whole body. All this, however, must be ensured without any sort of affectation.

- The art of living is more like wrestling than dancing, in as much as it, too, demands a firm and watchful stance against any unexpected onset.

- Nature has not blended mind so inextricably with body as to prevent it from establishing its own frontiers and controlling its own domain. It is perfectly possible to be godlike, even though unrecognized as such. Always keep that in mind; and also remember that the needs of a happy life are very few. Mastery of dialectics or physics may have eluded you, but that is no reason to despair of achieving freedom, self-respect, unselfishness, and obedience to the will of God.

· To live each day as though one's last, never flustered, never apathetic, never attitudinizing – here is the perfection of character.

· The gods, though they live for ever, feel no resentment at having to put up eternally with the generations of men and their misdeeds; nay more, they even show every possible care and concern for them. Are you, then, whose abiding is but for a moment, to lose patience – you who are yourself one of the culprits?

· When you have done a good action, and another has had the benefit of it, why crave for yet more in addition – applause for your kindness, or some favour in return – as the foolish do?

· No man tires of receiving benefits. But benefit comes from doing acts that accord with nature. Never tire, then, of receiving such benefits through the very act of conferring them.

- Universal Nature's impulse was to create an orderly world. It follows, then, that everything now happening must follow a logical sequence; if it were not so, the prime purpose towards which the impulses of the World-Reason are directed would be an irrational one. Remembrance of this will help you to face many things more calmly.

- Nothing can be good for a man unless it helps to make him just, self-disciplined, courageous, and independent; and nothing bad unless it has the contrary effect.

- You may break your heart, but men will still go on as before.

- You cannot hope to be a scholar. But what you can do is to curb arrogance; what you can do is to rise above pleasures and pains; you can be superior to the lure of popularity; you can keep your temper with the foolish and ungrateful, yes, and even care for them.

- Repentance is remorse for the loss of some helpful opportunity. Now, what is good is always helpful, and must be the concern of every good man; but an opportunity of pleasure is something no good man would ever repent of having let pass. It follows, therefore, that pleasure is neither good nor helpful.

- To change your mind and defer to correction is not to sacrifice your independence; for such an act is your own, in pursuance of your own impulse, your own judgement, and your own thinking.

- If the choice is yours, why do the thing? If another's, where are you to lay the blame for it? On gods? On atoms? Either would be insanity. All thoughts of blame are out of place. If you can, correct the offender; if not, correct the offence; if that too is impossible, what is the point of recriminations? Nothing is worth doing pointlessly.

- That which dies does not drop out of the world. Here it remains; and here too, therefore, it changes and is resolved into its several particles; that is, into the elements which go to form the universe and yourself. They themselves likewise undergo change, and yet from them comes no complaint.

- Everything – a horse, a vine – is created for some duty. This is nothing to wonder at: even the sun-god himself will tell you, 'There is a work that I am here to do,' and so will all the other sky-dwellers. For what task, then, were you yourself created? For pleasure? Can such a thought be tolerated?

- A man's true delight is to do the things he was made for. He was made to show goodwill to his kind, to rise above the promptings of his senses, to distinguish appearances from realities, and to pursue the study of universal Nature and her works.

- We have three relationships: one to this bodily shell which envelops us, one to the divine Cause which is the source of everything in all things, and one to our fellow-mortals around us.

- Pain must be an evil either to the body – in which case let the body speak for itself – or if not, to the soul. But the soul can always refuse to consider it an evil, and so keep its skies unclouded and its calm unruffled. For there is no decision, no impulse, no movement of approach or recoil, but must proceed from within the self; and into this self no evil can force its way.

- Erasing all fancies, keep on saying to yourself, 'It lies in my own hands to ensure that no viciousness, cupidity, or turmoil of any kind finds a home in this soul of mine; it lies with me to perceive all things in their true light, and to deal with each of them as it merits.' Remember this authority, which is nature's gift to you.

- Your every separate action should contribute towards an integrated life; and if each of them, so far as it can, does its part to this end, be satisfied; for that is something which nobody can prevent. 'There will be interferences from without,' you say? Even so, they will not affect the justice, prudence, and reasonableness of your intentions. 'No, but some kind of practical action may be prevented.' Perhaps; yet if you submit to the frustration with a good grace, and are sensible enough to accept what offers itself instead, you can substitute some alternative course which will be equally consistent with the integration we are speaking of.

- Accept modestly; surrender gracefully.

- You have perhaps seen a severed hand or foot, or a head lying by itself apart from its body. That is the state to which a man is doing his best to reduce himself, when he refuses to accept what befalls him and breaks away from his fellows, or when he acts for selfish ends alone. Then you become an outcast from the unity of 55

Nature; though born a part of it, you have cut yourself away with your own hand. Yet here is the beautiful thought: that it still lies in your own power to reunite yourself. No other part of creation has been so favoured by God with permission to come together again, after once being sundered and divided. Behold, then, his goodness, with which he has dignified man: he has put it in his power, not only initially to keep himself insepative from the whole, but afterwards, if separated, to return and be re-united and resume his membership as before.

· When the Nature of all things rational equipped each rational being with his powers, one of the faculties we received from her hand was this, that just as she herself transmutes every obstacle or opposition, fits it into its place in destiny's pattern, and assimilates it into herself, so a rational being has power to turn each hindrance into material for himself, and use it to set forward his own endeavours.

· Never confuse yourself by visions of an entire lifetime at once. That is, do not let your thoughts range over the whole multitude and variety of the misfortunes that may befall you, but rather, as you encounter each one, ask yourself, 'What is there unendurable, so insupportable, in this?' You will find that you are ashamed to admit defeat. Again, remember that it is not the weight of the future or the past that is pressing upon you, but ever that of the present alone. Even this burden, too, can be lessened if you confine it strictly to its own limits, and are severe enough with your mind's inability to bear such a trifle.

• In the constitution of a rational being, I find no virtue implanted for the combating of justice, but I do find self-control implanted for the combating of pleasure.

• Subtract your own notions of what you imagine to be painful, and then your self stands invulnerable. 'My self – what is it?' Your reason. 'But I am not all reason.' So be it; in that case, at least let your reason forbear to give pain to itself, and if another part of you is in trouble, let its thoughts about itself be its own concern.

• Take me and cast me where you will; I shall still be possessor of the divinity within me, serene and content so long as it can feel and act as becomes its constitution. Is the matter of such moment that my soul should be afflicted by it, and changed for the worse, to become a cowering craven thing, suppliant and spiritless? Could anything at all be of such consequence as that?

- No event can happen to a man but what is properly incidental to man's condition, nor to an ox, vine, or stone but what properly belongs to the nature of oxen, vines, and stones. Then if all things experience only what is customary and natural to them, why complain? The same Nature which is yours as well as theirs brings you nothing you cannot bear.

- If you are distressed by anything external, the pain is not due to the thing itself but to your own estimate of it; and this you have the power to revoke at any moment. If the cause of the trouble lies in your own character, set about reforming your principles; who is there to hinder you? If it is the failure to take some apparently sound course of action that is vexing you, then why not take it, instead of fretting? 'Because there is an insuperable obstacle in the way.' In that case, do not worry; the responsibility for inaction is not yours. 'But life is not worth living with this thing undone.' Why then, bid life a good-humoured farewell; accepting the frustration gracefully, and dying like any other man whose actions have not been inhibited.

- Remember that your higher Self becomes invincible when once it withdraws into itself and calmly refuses to act against its will, even though such resistance may be wholly irrational. How much more, then, when its decision is based on reason and circumspection! Thus a mind that is free from passion is a very citadel; man has no stronger fortress in which to seek shelter and defy every assault. Failure to perceive this is ignorance; but to perceive it, and still not to seek its refuge, is misfortune indeed.

- Never go beyond the sense of your original impressions. These tell you that such-and-such a person is speaking ill of you; that was their message; they did not go on to say it has done you any harm. I see my child is ill; my eyes tell me that, but they do not suggest that his life is in danger. Always, then, keep to the original impressions; supply no additions of your own, and you are safe. Or at least, add only a recognition of the great world-order by which all things are brought to pass.

- As your breathing partakes of the circumfluent air, so let your thinking partake of the circumfluent Mind. For there is a mental Force which, for him who can draw it to himself, is no less ubiquitous and all-pervading than is the atmosphere for him who can breathe it.

- He who fears death either fears to lose all sensation or fears new sensations. In reality, you will either feel nothing at all, and therefore nothing evil, or else, if you can feel any new sensations, you will be a new creature, and so will not have ceased to have life.

- Men exist for each other. Then either improve them, or put up with them.

- Injustice is a sin. Nature has constituted rational beings for their own mutual benefit, each to help his fellows according to their worth, and in no wise to do them hurt; and to contravene her will is plainly to sin against this eldest of all the deities. Untruthfulness, too, is a sin, and against the same goddess. For Nature is the nature of Existence itself; and existence connotes the kinship of all created beings. Truth is but another name for this Nature, the original creator of all true things. So, where a wilful lie is a sin because the deception is an act of injustice, an involuntary lie is also a sin because it is a discordant note in Nature's harmony, and creates mutinous disorder in an orderly universe. For mutinous indeed it is, when a man lets himself be carried, even involuntarily, into a position contrary to truth; seeing that he has so neglected the faculties Nature gave him that he is no longer able to distinguish the false from the true.

Again, it is a sin to pursue pleasure as a good and to

avoid pain as an evil. It is bound to result in complaints that Nature is unfair in her rewarding of vice and virtue; since it is the bad who are so often in enjoyment of pleasures and the means to obtain them, while pains and events that occasion pains descend upon the heads of the good. Besides, if a man is afraid of pain, he is afraid of something happening which will be part of the appointed order of things, and this is itself a sin; if he is bent on the pursuit of pleasure, he will not stop at acts of injustice, which again is manifestly sinful. No; when Nature herself makes no distinction – and if she did she would not have brought pains and pleasures into existence side by side – it behoves those who would follow in her footsteps to be like-minded and exhibit the same indifference. He therefore who does not view with equal unconcern pain or pleasure, death or life, fame or dishonour – all of them employed by Nature without any partiality – clearly commits a sin.

· Despise not death; smile, rather, at its coming; it is among the things that Nature wills. Like youth and age, like growth and maturity, like the advent of teeth, beard, and grey hairs, like begetting, pregnancy, and childbirth, like every other natural process that life's seasons bring us, so is our dissolution. Never, then, will a thinking man view death lightly, impatiently, or scornfully; he will wait for it as but one more of Nature's processes. Even as you await the baby's emergence from the womb of your wife, so await the hour when the little soul shall glide forth from its sheath.

But if your heart would have comfort of a simpler sort, then there is no better solace in the face of death than to think on the nature of the surroundings you are leaving, and the characters you will no longer have to mix with. Not that you must find these offensive; rather, your duty is to care for them and bear with them mildly; yet never forget that you are parting from men of far other principles than your own. One thing, if any, might have held you back and bound you to life; the chance of fellowship with kindred minds. But when you contemplate the weariness of an existence in company so discordant, you cry, 'Come quickly, Death, lest I too become forgetful of myself.'

- The sinner sins against himself; the wrongdoer wrongs himself, becoming the worse by his own action.

- Enough if your present opinion be grounded in conviction, your present action grounded in unselfishness, and your present disposition contented with whatever befalls you from without.

- Erase fancy; curb impulse; quench desire; let sovereign reason have the mastery.

- Everything bears fruit; man, God, the whole universe, each in its proper season. No matter that the phrase is restricted in common use to vines and such like. Reason, too, yields fruit, both for itself and for the world; since from it comes a harvest of other good things, themselves all bearing the stamp of reason.

- Work yourself hard, but not as if you were being made a victim, and not with any desire for sympathy or admiration. Desire one thing alone: that your actions or inactions alike should be worthy of a reasoning citizen.

- Today I have got myself out of all my perplexities; or rather, I have got the perplexities out of myself – for they were not without, but within; they lay in my own outlook.

- Everything is banal in experience, fleeting in duration, sordid in content; in all respects the same today as generations now dead and buried have found it to be.

- Facts stand wholly outside our gates; they are what they are, and no more; they know nothing about themselves, and they pass no judgement upon themselves. What is it, then, that pronounces the judgement? Our own guide and ruler, Reason.

· A rational and social being is not affected in himself for either better or worse by his feelings, but by his will; just as his outward behaviour, good or bad, is the product of will, not of feelings.

· Your own mind, the Mind of the universe, your neighbour's mind – be prompt to explore them all. Your own, so that you may shape it to justice; the universe's, that you may recollect what it is you are a part of; your neighbour's, that you may understand whether it is informed by ignorance or knowledge, and also may recognize that it is kin to your own.

· As a unit yourself, you help to complete the social whole; and similarly, therefore, your every action should help to complete the social life. Any action which is not related either directly or remotely to this social end disjoints that life, and destroys its unity. It is as much the act of a schismatic as when some citizen in a community does his utmost to dissociate himself from the general accord.

- Many of the anxieties that harass you are superfluous: being but creatures of your own fancy, you can rid yourself of them and expand into an ampler region, letting your thought sweep over the entire universe, contemplating the illimitable tracts of eternity, marking the swiftness of change in each created thing, and contrasting the brief span between birth and dissolution with the endless aeons that precede the one and the infinity that follows the other.

- A little while, and all that is before your eyes now will have perished. Those who witness its passing will go the same road themselves before long; and then what will there be to choose between the oldest grandfather and the baby that died in its cradle?

- Enough of this miserable way of life, these everlasting grumbles, these monkey antics. Why must you agitate yourself so? Nothing unprecedented is happening; so what is it that disturbs you? The form of it? Take a good look at it. The matter of it? Look well at that, too. Beyond form and matter, there is nothing more. Even at this late hour, set yourself to become a simpler and better man in the sight of the gods. For the mastering of that lesson, three years are as good as a hundred.

- When you are outraged by somebody's impudence, ask yourself at once, 'Can the world exist without impudent people?' It cannot; so do not ask for impossibilities. That man is simply one of the impudent whose existence is necessary to the world. Keep the same thought present, whenever you come across roguery, double-dealing or any other form of obliquity. You have only to remind yourself that the type is indispensable, and at once you will feel kindlier towards the individual. It is also helpful if you promptly recall what special quality Nature has given us to counter such particular faults. For there are antidotes with which she has provided us: gentleness to meet brutality, for example, and other correctives for other ills. Generally speaking, too, you have the opportunity of showing the culprit his blunder – for everyone who does wrong is failing of his proper objective, and is thereby a blunderer. Besides, what harm have you suffered? Nothing has been done by any of these victims of your irritation that could hurtfully affect your own mind; and it is in the mind alone that anything evil or damaging to the self can have reality. What is there wrong or surprising, after all, in a boor behaving boorishly? See then if it is not rather yourself you ought to blame, for not foreseeing that he would offend in this way. You, in virtue of your reason, had

every means for thinking it probable that he would do

so; you forgot this, and now his offence takes you by surprise. When you are indignant with anyone for his perfidy or ingratitude, turn your thoughts first and foremost upon yourself. For the error is clearly your own, if you have put any faith in the good faith of a man of that stamp, or, when you have done him a kindness, if it was not done unreservedly and in the belief that the action would be its own full reward. Once you have done a man a service, what more would you have? Is it not enough to have obeyed the laws of your own nature, without expecting to be paid for it? That is like the eye demanding a reward for seeing, or the feet for walking. It is for that very purpose that they exist; and they have their due in doing what they were created to do. Similarly, man is born for deeds of kindness; and when he has done a kindly action, or otherwise served the common welfare, he has done what he was made for, and has received his quittance.

• O soul of mine, will you never be good and sincere, all one, all open, visible to the beholder more clearly than even your encompassing body of flesh? Will you never taste the sweetness of a loving and affectionate heart? Will you never be filled full and unwanting; craving nothing, yearning for no creature or thing to minister to your pleasures, no prolongation of days to enjoy them, 67 no place or country or pleasant clime or sweet human company? When will you be content with your present state, happy in all about you, persuaded that all things are yours, that all comes from the gods, and that all is and shall be well with you, so long as it is their good pleasure and ordained by them for the safety and welfare of that perfect living Whole – so good, so just, so beautiful – which gives life to all things, upholding and enfolding them, and at their dissolution gathering them into Itself so that yet others of their kind may spring forth? Will you never be fit for such fellowship with gods and men as to have no syllable of complaint against them, and no syllable of reproach from them?

- Pay heed to what your particular nature requires of you, like one who is wholly under great Nature's governance. Do it and accept it, provided always that it promise no harm to your physical nature, and give assent to them all, unless they in turn promise harm to the rational nature (and by the rational is directly implied the social as well). Observe these rules, without wasting pains on other things.

- Whatever befalls, Nature has either prepared you to face it or she has not. If something untoward happens which is within your powers of endurance, do not resent it, but bear it as she has enabled you to do. Should it exceed those powers, still do not give way to resentment; for its victory over you will put an end to its own existence. Remember, however, that in fact Nature has given you the ability to bear anything which your own judgement succeeds in declaring bearable and endurable by regarding it as a point of self-interest and duty to do so.

• If a man makes a slip, admonish him gently and show him his mistake. If you fail to convince him, blame yourself, or else blame nobody.

• Whatever may happen to you was prepared for you in advance from the beginning of time. In the woven tapestry of causation, the thread of your being had been intertwined from all time with that particular incident.

• If you claim for yourself such epithets as good, modest, truthful, clear-minded, right-minded, high-minded, be careful not to belie them; and if you should happen to forfeit them, lose no time in recovering them again. But remember that 'clear-mindedness' ought to suggest to you a discriminating consideration of each separate detail and a watchful attention to it; 'right-mindedness' a willing acceptance of all that Nature allots you; and 'high-mindedness' an elevation of the intellect above the workings of the flesh, be they smooth or harsh, and above vainglory, death or any other such distractions. Live up to these designations – though without craving to have them applied to you by others – and you will be a different man and enter upon a different life. To go on in your present state, continuing to be torn and soiled by an existence like this, is the way of a fool and a faint-heart; it smacks of the swordsman who has been mangled by beasts in the arena and covered with blood and bruises, and yet still pleads to be kept till the morrow, when he will only be flung again, wounds and all, to the same teeth and claws. So step on board this little raft of attributes, and if you can contrive it, stay there as though transported to the Isles of the Blest. But if you feel yourself drifting and unable to hold your course, pluck up heart and make for some quiet haven where you will be able to hold your own; or even bid farewell to life altogether, not in a passion but simply, freely, and unassumingly, with at least this one success in life to your credit, a seemly departure from it. In order to keep those attributes ever in mind, it will help greatly not to forget the gods: to remember that what they desire is not to be flattered but that everything which has reason should become like themselves; and also to recollect that a fig-tree is that which does a fig-

tree's work, a dog that which does a dog's, a bee a bee's
– and a man a man's.

· Day by day the buffoonery, quarrelling, timidity, sloth-
fulness, and servility that surround you will conspire to
efface from your mind those hallowed maxims it appre-
hends so unphilosophically and dismisses so carelessly.
What duty requires of you is to observe each single
thing and perform each action in such a manner that,
while the practical demands of a situation are fully met,
the powers of thought are at the same time fully exer-
cised; and also to maintain (in reserve, but never lost to
sight) the self-confidence of one who has mastered
every relevant detail. Are you never going to attain to
the happiness of a real integrity and dignity? Of an
understanding which comprehends the inmost being of
each thing, its place in the world-order, the term of its
natural existence, the structure of its composition, and
to whom it belongs or who has the power of bestowing
or withdrawing it?

· Make a habit of regularly observing the universal process of change; be assiduous in your attention to it, and
school yourself thoroughly in this branch of study;
there is nothing more elevating to the mind. For when a
man realizes that at any moment he may have to leave

everything behind him and depart from the company of his fellows, he casts off the body and thenceforward dedicates himself wholly to the service of justice in his personal actions and compliance with Nature in all else. No thought is wasted on what others may say or think of him or practise against him; two things alone suffice him, justice in his daily doings and contentment with all fate's apportionings. Every care, every distraction is laid aside; his only ambition is to walk in the straight paths of law, and by so doing to become a follower of God.

- To Nature, whence all things come and whither all return, the cry of the humble and well-instructed heart is, 'Give as thou wilt, take back as thou wilt;' yet uttered with no heroics, but in pure obedience and goodwill.

- Waste no more time arguing what a good man should be. Be one.

- For every man and every thing, that which Nature brings makes for their own good; moreover, makes for their good at the precise moment when it is brought.

· Whatever you take in hand, pause at every step to ask

yourself, 'Is it the thought of forfeiting this that makes me dread death?'

- When another's fault offends you, turn to yourself and consider what similar shortcomings are found in you. Do you, too, find your good in riches, pleasure, reputation, or such like? Think of this, and your anger will soon be forgotten in the reflection that he is only acting under pressure; what else could he do? Alternatively, if you are able, contrive his release from that pressure.

- What is the very best that can be said or done with the materials at your disposal? Be it what it may, you have the power to say it or do it; let there be no pretence that you are not a free agent.

- The business of a healthy eye is to see everything that is visible, not to demand no colour but green, for that merely marks a disordered vision. Likewise hearing and scent, if healthy, should be alert for all kinds of sounds and odours, and a healthy stomach for all manner of meats, like a mill which accepts whatever grist it was fashioned to grind. In the same way, then, a healthy mind ought to be prepared for anything that may befall. A mind crying 'O that my children may be spared,' or 'O that the world might ring with the praises of my every act,' is an eye craving for greenery, or a tooth craving for softness.

- At every action, no matter by whom performed, make it a practice to ask yourself, 'What is his object in doing this?' But begin with yourself; put this question to yourself first of all.

- Remember, it is the secret force hidden deep within us that manipulates our strings; there lies the voice of persuasion, there the very life, there, we might even say, is the man himself. Never confuse it in your imagination with its surrounding case of flesh, or the organs adhering thereto, which save that they grow upon the body, are as much mere instruments as the carpenter's axe. Without the agency that prompts or restrains their motions, the parts themselves are of no more service than her shuttle to the weaver, his pen to the writer, or his whip to the wagoner.

- The properties of a rational soul are these. She can contemplate herself, analyse herself, make of herself what she will, herself enjoy the fruit she bears (whereas the fruit produced by trees, like its counterpart produced by animals, is enjoyed by others), and always
have her work perfectly complete at whatever moment

our life reaches its appointed limit. For, unlike dances or plays or such like, where if they are suddenly cut short the performance as a whole is left imperfect, the soul, no matter at what stage arrested, will have her task complete to her own satisfaction, and be able to say, 'I am in the fullest possession of mine own.' Moreover, she can encompass the whole universe at will, both its own structure and the void surrounding it, and can reach out into eternity, embracing and comprehending the great cyclic renewals of creation, and thereby perceiving that future generations will have nothing new to witness, even as our forefathers beheld nothing more than we of today, but that if a man comes to his fortieth year, and has any understanding at all, he has virtually seen – thanks to their similarity – all possible happenings, both past and to come. Finally, the qualities of the rational soul include love of neighbours, truthfulness, modesty, and a reverence for herself before all else; and since this last is one of the qualities of law also, it follows that the principle of rationality is one and the same as the principle of justice.

· Happy the soul which, at whatever moment the call comes for release from the body, is equally ready to face extinction, dispersion, or survival. Such preparedness, however, must be the outcome of its own decision; a decision not prompted by mere contumacy, but formed with deliberation and gravity and, if it is to be convincing to others, with an absence of all heroics.

- Though men may hinder you from following the paths of reason, they can never succeed in deflecting you from sound action; but make sure that they are equally unsuccessful in destroying your charitable feelings towards them. You must defend both positions alike: your firmness in decision and action, and at the same time your gentleness to those who try to obstruct or otherwise molest you. It would be as great a weakness to give way to your exasperation with them as it would be to abandon your course of action and be browbeaten into surrender. In either event the post of duty is deserted; in the one case through lack of courage, and in the other through alienation from men who are your natural brothers and friends.

- The soul attains her perfectly rounded form when she is neither straining out after something nor shrinking back into herself; neither disseminating herself piecemeal nor yet sinking down in collapse; but is bathed in a radiance which reveals to her the world and herself in their true colours.

- Will any one sneer at me? That will be his concern; mine will be to ensure that nothing I do or say shall deserve the sneer. Will he perhaps hate me? Again, his concern. Mine, to be in friendship and charity with all men, ready to show this very man himself where he is mistaken, and to do so without recrimination or ostentatious forbearance. That is the right spirit for a man to have within him; he should never be seen by the gods in the act of harbouring a grudge or making a grievance of his sufferings. What ill can touch you if you follow the proper laws of your being and accept moment by moment whatever great Nature deems opportune, like a true man who is bent on furthering by any and every means the welfare of the world?

- How hollow and insincere it sounds when someone says, 'I am determined to be perfectly straightforward with you.' Why, man, what is all this? The thing needs no prologue; it will declare itself. It should be written on your forehead, it should echo in the tones of your voice, it should shine out in a moment from your eyes, just as a single glance from the beloved tells all to the lover. Sincerity and goodness ought to have their own unmistakable odour, so that one who encounters this becomes straightway aware of it despite himself. A candour affected is a dagger concealed. The feigned 77 friendship of the wolf is the most contemptible of all, and to be shunned beyond everything. A man who is truly good and sincere and well-meaning will show it by his looks, and no one can fail to see it.

- The good life can be achieved to perfection by any soul capable of showing indifference to the things that are themselves indifferent. This can be done by giving careful scrutiny first to the elements that compose them, and then to the things themselves; bearing also in mind that none of them is responsible for the opinion we form of it. They make no approaches to us, they remain stationary; it is we who produce judgements about them, and proceed to inscribe these, so to speak, in our minds; despite the fact that it is perfectly in our power either to inscribe nothing at all, or at least to delete promptly anything that may have inscribed itself unawares. Moreover, you must remember that there will not be much more time in which to give heed to these matters, and that your race will soon be run. Do not be aggrieved, then, if things are not always to your liking. As long as they are in accord with nature, be glad of them, and do not make difficulties; if they are not, then find out what your own nature itself enjoins, and make the best of your way towards that; for a man is always justified in seeking his own good.

- There are four aberrations of your soul's helmsman which you must constantly guard against, and suppress whenever detected. Say to them one by one, 'This is a thought which is not necessary,' 'This is one which would undermine fellowship,' 'This is not the voice of my true self' (for to speak anything but your true sentiments, remember, is of all things the most misplaced), and, fourthly, when you are tempted into self-reproach, 'This would prove the divine element in me to have been discomfited and forced to its knees by the ignoble and perishable flesh with its gross conceptions.'

- If a man's life has no consistent and uniform aim, it cannot itself remain consistent or uniform. Yet that statement does not go far enough unless you can also add something of what the aim should be. Now, it is not upon the whole range of the things which are generally assumed to be good that we find uniformity of opinion to exist, but only upon things of a certain kind: namely, those which affect the welfare of society. Accordingly, the aim we should propose to ourselves must be the benefit of our fellows and the community. Whoso directs his every effort to this will be imparting a uniformity to all his actions, and so will achieve consistency with himself.

- 'While you are kissing your child,' Epictetus once said, 'murmur under your breath, tomorrow it may be dead.' 'Ominous words,' they told him. 'Not at all,' said he, 'but only signifying an act of nature. Would it be ominous to speak of the gathering of ripe corn?'

- All the blessings which you pray to obtain hereafter could be yours today, if you did not deny them to yourself. You have only to have done with the past altogether, commit the future to providence, and simply seek to direct the present hour aright into the paths of holiness and justice: holiness, by a loving acceptance of your apportioned lot, since Nature produced it for you and you for it: justice, in your speech by a frank and straightforward truthfulness, and in your acts by a respect for law and for every man's rights. Allow yourself, too, no hindrance from the malice, misconceptions or slanders of others, nor yet from any sensations this fleshy frame may feel; its afflicted part will look to itself. The hour for your departure draws near; if you will but forget all else and pay sole regard to the helmsman of your soul and the divine spark within you – if you will but exchange your fear of having to end your life some day for a fear of failing even to begin it on nature's true principles – you can yet become a man, worthy of the universe that gave you birth, instead of a stranger in your own homeland, bewildered by each day's happenings as though by wonders unlooked for, and ever hanging upon this one or the next.

- God views the inner minds of men, stripped of every material sheath and husk and dross. Acting through his thought alone, he makes contact solely with that in them which is an outflow from himself. School yourself to do likewise, and you will be spared many a distraction; for who that looks past this fleshly covering will ever harass himself with visions of raiment, housing, reputation, or any of the rest of life's costume and scenery?

- I often marvel how it is that though each man loves himself beyond all else, he should yet value his own opinion of himself less than that of others. Assuredly if some god or sage counsellor were to stand beside him and bid him harbour no thought or purpose in his heart without straightway publishing it abroad, he could not endure it for so much as a single day. So much more regard have we for our neighbours' judgement of us than for our own.

- Can the gods, who have contrived all else so well and so benevolently, have overlooked this one thing, that even eminently virtuous men, men in the closest correspondence with the divine and living in intimate union with it through their good works and devotion, should know no re-birth after their death, but be doomed to utter extinction? However, should this indeed be their lot, rest assured that if there had been need for some different plan, it would have been so ordained; had it accorded with Nature, Nature would have brought it to pass.

- Meditate upon what you ought to be in body and soul when death overtakes you; meditate upon the brevity of life, and the measureless gulfs of eternity behind it and before, and upon the frailty of everything material.

- Look at the inmost causes of things, stripped of their husks; note the intentions that underlie actions; study the essences of pain, pleasure, death, glory; observe how man's disquiet is all of his own making, and how troubles come never from another's hand, but like all else are creatures of our own opinion.

- In the management of your principles, take example by the pugilist, not the swordsman. One puts down his blade and has to pick it up again; the other is never without his hand, and so needs only to clench it.

- If it is not the right thing to do, never do it; if it is not the truth, never say it. Keep your impulses in hand.

- Always look at the whole of a thing. Find what it is that makes its impression on you, then open it up and dissect it into cause, matter, purpose, and the length of time before it must end.

- Everything is but what your opinion makes it; and that opinion lies with yourself. Renounce it when you will, and at once you have rounded the foreland and all is calm; a tranquil sea, a tideless haven.

- When an operation, no matter of what sort, is brought to a close at the right moment, the stoppage does it no harm and the agent himself is no worse for discontinuing his action. So if life itself – which is nothing but the totality of all our operations – also ceases when the time comes, it takes no hurt by its mere cessation, nor is he adversely affected who thus brings the whole series of his operations to its timely conclusion. But the proper hour and term are fixed by nature: if not by a man's own nature – as, for example, through old age – then at all events by great Nature herself, by whose continuous renewing of her every part the universe remains forever

young and vigorous. Whatever serves the purpose of
the Whole is kept always fair and blooming. It follows,
then, that the ending of his life can be no evil to a man
– for, being a thing outside his control and innocent of
all self-seeking, there is nothing in it to degrade him –
nay, it is even a good, inasmuch as for the universe it is
something opportune, serviceable and in keeping with
all else. Thus, by following the way of God and being
at one with him in thought, man is borne onward by
the divine hand.

• When you let yourself feel resentment at a thing, you
forget that nothing can come about except in obedience
to Nature; that any misconduct in the matter was none
of yours; and moreover, that this is the only way in
which things have always happened, will always happen,
and do always happen. You are forgetting, too, the
closeness of man's brotherhood with his kind; a brotherhood not of blood or human seed, but of a common
intelligence; and that this intelligence in every man is
God, an emanation from the deity. You forget that
nothing is properly a man's own, for even his child, his
body, his soul itself, all come from this same God; also,
that all things depend upon opinion; also, that the
passing moment is all that a man can ever live or
lose.

- How is my soul's helmsman going about his task? For in that lies everything. All else, within my control or beyond it, is dead bones and vapour.

- When a man finds his sole good in that which the appointed hour brings him; when he cares not if his actions be many or few, so they accord with strict reason; when it matters nought to him whether his glimpse of this world be long or fleeting – not death itself can be a thing of terror for him.

- O man, citizenship of this great world-city has been yours. Whether for five years or fivescore, what is that to you? Whatever the law of that city decrees is fair to one and all alike. Wherein, then, is your grievance? You are not ejected from the city by an unjust judge or tyrant, but by the selfsame Nature which brought you into it; just as when an actor is dismissed by the manager who engaged him. 'But I have played on more than three of the five acts.' Just so; in your drama of life, three acts are all the play. Its point of completeness is determined by him who formerly sanctioned your creation, and today sanctions your dissolution. Neither of those decisions lay within yourself. Pass on your way, then, with a smiling face, under the smile of him who bids you go.

PENGUIN 60s

READ MORE IN PENGUIN

For complete information about books available from Penguin and how to order them, please write to us at the appropriate address below. Please note that for copyright reasons the selection of books varies from country to country.

IN THE UNITED KINGDOM: Please write to *Dept. JC, Penguin Books Ltd, FREEPOST, West Drayton, Middlesex UB7 0BR*.

If you have any difficulty in obtaining a title, please send your order with the correct money, plus ten per cent for postage and packaging, to *PO Box No. 11, West Drayton, Middlesex UB7 0BR*.

IN THE UNITED STATES: Please write to *Consumer Sales, Penguin USA, P.O. Box 999, Dept. 17109, Bergenfield, New Jersey 07621-0120*. VISA and MasterCard holders call 1-800-253-6476 to order all Penguin titles.

IN CANADA: Please write to *Penguin Books Canada Ltd, 10 Alcorn Avenue, Suite 300, Toronto, Ontario M4V 3B2*.

IN AUSTRALIA: Please write to *Penguin Books Australia Ltd, P.O. Box 257, Ringwood, Victoria 3134*.

IN NEW ZEALAND: Please write to *Penguin Books (NZ) Ltd, Private Bag 102902, North Shore Mail Centre, Auckland 10*.

IN INDIA: Please write to *Penguin Books India Pvt Ltd, 706 Eros Apartments, 56 Nehru Place, New Delhi 110 019*.

IN THE NETHERLANDS: Please write to *Penguin Books Netherlands bv, Postbus 3507, NL-1001 AH Amsterdam*.

IN GERMANY: Please write to *Penguin Books Deutschland GmbH, Metzlerstrasse 26, 60594 Frankfurt am Main*.

IN SPAIN: Please write to *Penguin Books S. A., Bravo Murillo 19, 1o B, 28015 Madrid*.

IN ITALY: Please write to *Penguin Italia s.r.l., Via Felice Casati 20, I-20124 Milano*.

IN FRANCE: Please write to *Penguin France S. A., 17 rue Lejeune, F-31000 Toulouse*.

IN JAPAN: Please write to *Penguin Books Japan, Ishikiribashi Building, 2-5-4, Suido, Bunkyo-ku, Tokyo 112*.

IN GREECE: Please write to *Penguin Hellas Ltd, Dimocritou 3, GR-106 71 Athens*.

IN SOUTH AFRICA: Please write to *Longman Penguin Southern Africa (Pty) Ltd, Private Bag X08, Bertsham 2013*.